HOMOSEXUALITY
GUIDANCE FOR COMMUNITY CONVERSATION
AND THE CHURCH

About the "In All Things Charity" Series

John Wesley is often credited with the saying, "In essentials unity. In non-essentials liberty. In all things charity."

As the world becomes more religiously pluralistic and societies and cultures grow more contentious and divided it will behoove the church to gain clarity in its discernment of the distinction between essentials and non-essentials. We must not shrink back from boldly articulating the core truths of the Christian faith. At the same time, we must grow in the quality of our character as our very conversations witness to the gospel in the presence of a watching world. Said simply, our relationships within the church are the barometer of our witness to the world.

Jesus minced no words when he told his disciples that the authenticity of their association with him would be known only by the quality of their love for one another. Later in prayer he would connect the loving unity of the church to the believability of the gospel. See John 17.

The Apostle Paul, in the celebrated thirteenth chapter of his first letter to the Corinthian Church, in essence tells us the absence of charity, or love, signals failure.

As a publisher, Seedbed does not want to steer clear of the difficult subjects of our time. Nor do we want to agitate the church with unnecessary controversy. For this reason, Seedbed created the "In All Things Charity" series. The series will contain books across a range of challenging issues. For the series we are selecting authors whom we believe embody the variety of character which enables them to demonstrate confidence in their point of view with truthful love in their approach.

HOMOSEXUALITY
GUIDANCE FOR COMMUNITY CONVERSATION
AND THE CHURCH

HOWARD A. SNYDER

Homosexuality and the Church:
Guidance for Community Conversation

Printed in the United States of America

Paperback ISBN: 978-1-62824-154-9
Mobi ISBN: 978-1-62824-155-6
ePub ISBN: 978-1-62824-156-3
uPDF ISBN: 978-1-62824-157-0

Library of Congress Control Number: 2014951086

Cover design by Andrew Dragos
Page design by PerfecType, Nashville, TN

SEEDBED PUBLISHING
Franklin, Tennessee
seedbed.com
SOWING FOR A GREAT AWAKENING

To my grandchildren and prospective
great-grandchildren—that they and future generations
may walk in Jesus' love and truth.

Other Books by Howard A. Snyder

The Problem of Wineskins: Church Structure in a Technological Age
InterVarsity Press, 1975

The Community of the King
InterVarsity Press, 1977. Rev. ed., 2004

The Radical Wesley: The Patterns and Practices of a Movement Maker
Seedbed Press, 2014

Liberating the Church: The Ecology of Church and Kingdom
InterVarsity Press, 1983

Kingdom, Church, and World: Biblical Themes for Today
Wipf & Stock, 2002

The Divided Flame: Wesleyans and the Charismatic Movement
(with Daniel Runyon) Wipf & Stock, 2011

Signs of the Spirit: How God Reshapes the Church
Zondervan Press, 1989

Models of the Kingdom
Abingdon Press, 1991

EarthCurrents: The Struggle for the World's Soul
Abingdon Press, 1995

Decoding the Church: Mapping the DNA of Christ's Body (with Daniel Runyon)
Baker Books, 2002

*"Live While You Preach": The Autobiography of Methodist Revivalist and
Abolitionist John Wesley Redfield (1810–1863)* (editor)
Scarecrow Press, 2006

Populist Saints: B. T. and Ellen Roberts and the First Free Methodists
Eerdmans, 2006

Yes in Christ: Wesleyan Reflections on Gospel, Mission, and Culture
Tyndale Series in Wesleyan History and Theology, Vol. 2.
Toronto: Clements Academic, 2011

Salvation Means Creation Healed: The Ecology of Sin and Grace
(with Joel Scandrett) Cascade Books, 2011

Contents

Foreword

One of the foundational problems with the contemporary discussion on same-sex marriage is that the church has lost the debate before the first exchange of ideas takes place. This is because the underlying presuppositions of the dialogue are never properly disclosed. For example, the actual biblical teaching regarding marriage is utterly incomprehensible to the wider culture. If you read Christian interactions about same-sex marriage, it is clear that the church has largely abandoned the notion that there is a divine design to marriage. In short, we have a priori accepted the culture's view of marriage: namely, that it is a legal arrangement that allows two people to fulfill each other's emotional and sexual needs and desires. Personal choice and autonomous notions of personal fulfillment are just a few of the values that fit neatly within the larger utilitarian framework of the modern understanding of marriage. Today, marriage has become commodified along with the rest of the culture, as even social relationships are often reduced to measurable economic and emotional exchange units.

In contrast, the Scriptures posit a covenantal view of marriage that is unitive, becoming cocreators with God, modeling the redemptive, sacrificial self-donation of God Himself, and ultimately designed to reflect the Trinity itself. Much of this is lost in the modern debate.

In this reflection, Dr. Howard Snyder has brought considerable clarity to the ongoing conversation about the church's response to same-sex marriage. This reflection is highly pastoral, seeking to listen, as well as respond, in a way that is faithful to the teaching of Scripture and pastorally sensitive to those who may disagree. This piece originated as a blog and continues in that mode as it seeks to interact with various responders in the true spirit of pastoral care and honest dialogue. But Snyder also seeks to address the whole question within the larger biblical, historical, and theological framework, which is essential if we are to have this discussion, inside the church, on proper grounds. I commend this reflection. It will help us all to be more faithful witnesses to God's design for marriage.

Timothy C. Tennent, PhD
President, Asbury Theological Seminary
Professor of World Christianity

Introduction

Let's start with Jesus. That's the best place to start in a book about homosexuality and the church.

What Jesus Did

One day a Pharisee invited Jesus to dinner. As Jesus and other guests were reclining and dining, "a woman of the city" quietly and boldly walked into the all-male gathering and stood behind Jesus, at his feet. The Pharisees recognized the woman; she was a "sinner." She held a white translucent perfume vase, and she was weeping.

The woman knelt behind Jesus. Tears dropped on his feet as she kissed them, then dried them with her long hair. She spread perfumed ointment on both feet and sat there, crying.

Jesus' host was aghast. "Jesus should know better," he thought. "He's letting a sinner touch him!"

Jesus looked at his host and distracted him with a story about a man who was forgiven of a big debt he couldn't pay. The forgiven debtor was immensely relieved and grateful.

Jesus made his point. "Look at this woman," he said. "She treated me better than you have. Her many sins are forgiven, for she has come to me in great love."

Then Jesus told the woman, "Your faith has saved you; your sins are forgiven. Go in peace" (Luke 7:36–50).

On another day Jesus arrived early at the Jerusalem temple to teach. Already a crowd was waiting. Jesus sat down and began.

But he was interrupted. Some Jewish officials walked up with a woman in tow. "Look at this!" they said. "This woman was caught in the very act of adultery! Should we stone her, as the law says?" They were, of course, trying to trap Jesus; the woman was their pawn.

Jesus didn't look at them or the woman. Instead, he bent over and with his finger wrote words in the dust. The accusers insisted that Jesus make a judgment.

Jesus straightened up and looked at the men. "OK," he said. "Let the sinless ones among you start the stoning."

Sudden silence. Then the men began slinking away. The woman stood alone before Jesus. "Well," he said, "where are your accusers? Is no one left to throw a stone?"

"No one, Sir," she said.

"Well, I won't either. Go home, but don't sin anymore" (John 8:1–11).

A final incident: Jesus was resting at the well just outside the Samaritan town of Sychar while his disciples went off to buy some lunch. A woman walked up to the well and began to draw some water, carefully avoiding Jesus.

Jesus said to her, "Give me a drink!"

The woman looked at him. "You're a Jewish man; I'm a Samaritan woman! How can you ask me for a drink?"

Jesus said, "If you knew who I am, you would ask me for a drink! I would give you fresh, flowing water."

"What?" she said. "You don't even have a pail, and the well is deep! Where can you get flowing water? You think you're greater than our ancestor Jacob who dug this well?"

Jesus said he had water that would be "a spring gushing up to eternal life."

"Give me some!"

Jesus replied, "First go get your husband." When the woman said she didn't have one, Jesus said, "Right. Actually you've had five, and you're not married to the man you're living with right now."

Ouch! She changed the subject. "So, you're a prophet. We worship right here, but you Jews say we have to go to Jerusalem."

Jesus said, "It's not a question of here or there. God wants people to worship him from the heart—wherever. Right now."

The woman paused. "Well," she said, "I know Messiah is coming. . . ."

Jesus said, "I'm the one."

Just then Jesus' disciples returned and were dumbfounded to find Jesus carrying on with a Samaritan woman. But she hurried back to the city, forgetting her water jar. "Come and see the amazing man I just met!" she told everyone she saw. "Is this the Messiah?"

A crowd of people streamed out to the well. Many heard for themselves, and believed: "This is truly the Savior of the world!" (John 4:7–42).

The Point

None of these stories mention homosexuality. Adultery and promiscuity, yes, but not homosexuality.

Yet these stories offer a key insight and larger principle. Transposed to today, they could just as well be about encounters with homosexual persons. The stories teach us three things.

First: Unchained love for the other, the outcast, the discriminated-against, the different. Love demonstrated in actions, not just attitudes. Readiness to talk; to converse; to relate one-to-one. Jesus speaks lovingly to all three women. Everyone was surprised, including them!

Second: In these encounters, Jesus takes the side of "the other" rather than the condemners and excluders.

Third: In none of these encounters does Jesus endorse ungodly behavior. To the woman caught in adultery: "Go, and sin no more." To the "woman of the city": "Your sins are forgiven." To the Samaritan woman Jesus clearly implies: Worship God in spirit and truth, and put your private life in order.

What unites these three points is character—the holy Trinitarian loving character of God, made earthy and visible in Jesus.

Here is the principle: *Unrestricted love without compromise on moral or doctrinal truth as revealed in Scripture.*

Fade to Today

If we begin with Jesus, we should begin here whenever we engage questions of sexual ethics, including same-sex attraction and behavior.

Public opinion about homosexuality has shifted dramatically over the past decade, especially in the

United States. Should the Church of Jesus Christ fall in line?

Christian views and practices actually vary a lot from church to church and from place to place. Yet historically the Christian Church has largely agreed that homosexual practice is inconsistent with faithful Christian practice. This has been the Christian consensus since New Testament days.

What about today?

Jeff Chu raises the issue sharply in his book, *Does Jesus Really Love Me? A Gay Christian's Pilgrimage in Search of God in America*. Through interviews and stories, Chu displays the range of viewpoints among Christians in the United States. Much of it is painful reading. Chu shows how unkind and un-understanding sincere Christians can be.[1]

Yet what strikes me about Chu's book is an unstated assumption. Chu seems truly offended by the very idea that there could be a Christian counterculture that disagrees with the growing national consensus and lovingly opposes homosexual practice out of loyalty to Jesus Christ.

So, what is at stake here? Does homosexuality involve core issues of Christian belief? Or is homosexuality essentially a question of human rights and individual freedom—the current hotspot in the long battle that progressively has opened freedom to slaves and sought equality for women and other victims of discrimination?

Popular opinion has already answered the question: Yes, it's the current civil rights issue. If so, given U.S. commitment to equal rights, the issue is settled.

But biblical Christians have a broader lens. We affirm the equality of all humans created in God's image. We ought to work to end oppression and injustice; we ought to help everyone enjoy the full freedom of the gospel of Jesus Christ. And we must, above all else, be loyal to Jesus and his teachings.

What then about homosexuality, and homosexual practice?

The Shape of the Argument

I addressed this question in a blog on Asbury Seminary's online *Seedbed* site in September 2012. The piece sparked lots of comments. As a result, I have now expanded the original short article into this longer essay, with additional points and clarifications in light of feedback received.

I personally struggle with the many issues surrounding homosexuality. How are we to understand these issues as faithful Jesus followers? How do we express gospel truth and love—both, not one or the other—in relating to people for whom this is a matter of crucial, often wrenching, personal concern?

I have come to believe that homosexuality is indeed a key issue for Christian faith and witness. It is more than a question of rights and freedom. It involves fundamental issues of Christian doctrine, as I will explain. Note that by *homosexuality* I mean not only same-sex attraction or relationships, but also a range of related issues.

I discuss this matter not to create controversy nor to oppose those with other views. I write mainly to help those who, like myself, want to think the matter through faithfully, scripturally, and lovingly. In fact, I felt I needed to ponder this for myself and come to my own settled view—which includes leaving space for aspects of this matter which remain unresolved (for example, the role of genetic factors).

Throughout the discussion, I am assuming the important distinction between *preference* and *practice*. Our concern here (as John Stott phrased it) "is homosexual practice (for which a person is responsible) and not homosexual orientation or preference (for which he or she is not responsible)."[2]

I divide the discussion into five short sections. First, I give four key reasons why homosexual practice is incompatible with faithful Christian discipleship. Second, I discuss the question of homosexual practice in relation to essential Christian doctrine. Third, I offer a biblical case study that clarifies the fundamental issues of biblical interpretation (hermeneutics) involved. Fourth, I ask whether people in committed same-sex relationships can at the same time be faithful Christian disciples. Finally, I respond to a range of questions raised by my original blog and subsequently, in question-and-answer form.

HOMOSEXUALITY

GUIDANCE FOR COMMUNITY CONVERSATION

AND THE CHURCH

[Section One]

Four Key Biblical and Theological Considerations

Here are four reasons that the acceptance or nonacceptance of homosexual practice is a key issue for Christian faith.

1. The Witness of Scripture

What does the Bible teach? For Christians, this and Jesus' own example is the starting point.

In his book *Slaves, Women & Homosexuals: Exploring the Hermeneutics of Cultural Analysis*, biblical scholar William J. Webb makes a crucial point. Webb carefully examines the "direction of movement" within the

Bible on a range of issues "as a criterion for interpreting biblical truth today."[1] His particular test cases, as his title indicates, are slavery, women, and homosexuality.

Regarding slaves and women, Webb shows that the trajectory of biblical revelation is consistently toward greater freedom: less restriction and discrimination. As he puts it, biblical texts dealing with women and slaves gradually become "generally 'less restrictive' or [show a] 'softening' relative to the broader culture." But in contrast "the homosexuality texts are 'more restrictive' or [demonstrate] 'hardening' relative to the surrounding environment." Other sound principles of interpretation confirm this, he notes.[2]

In other words: the Bible reveals a "trajectory" toward greater freedom (less restriction) for women and slaves—both within Scripture and in relation to the surrounding culture. In contrast, no such trajectory is found in the case of homosexual practice. In all the Bible, both Old Testament and New, homosexual practice is forbidden and viewed as sin.

Webb states this more explicitly in the book's conclusion: "*the homosexual texts are in a different category than the women and slavery texts. The former are almost entirely transcultural in nature, while the latter are heavily bound by culture.*" In other words, homosexuality involves a more basic issue than mere cultural considerations.

This insight provides a decisive answer "to homo-sexual advocates who say the cultural dimensions of the women and slavery texts should lead to the acceptance of homosexuality." Analysis of the entire Bible reveals a "fundamental difference between the women's issue and the homosexuality issue."[3]

So homosexuality is fundamentally different from the issues of slavery and women's roles. Homosexuality goes to the very heart of human identity. Thus from the Christian perspective, it is not, at heart, a civil rights issue.[4]

Within civil society, however, things are different. The rights of homosexuals *is* a legitimate issue. But the Bible (and the church) holds to a different and higher standard of moral behavior, by definition, than does a modern civil society, which is by law neutral and "secular" with regard to religion.

The point: same-sex unions in the church and in civil society are two quite different matters. There is no reason Christians should think that the standards and morality of civil society should be those of the Christian community! In fact, the Bible consistently teaches just the opposite. For we are followers of Jesus Christ, not of the ways of the present age or "the basic principles of the world" (Gal. 4:3 NIV).[5]

The early Christians understood this very well. They said Jesus, not Caesar, was king. A different drummer. A different Shepherd. A different King and community.

Christians know from Scripture that homosexual relations (whether committed or promiscuous) are a result of the Fall, of sin. This is not true of licit heterosexual relations, which are God-given. In this limited sense, homosexual sin and heterosexual sin are different. Homosexual practice derives from sin in ways that gender differentiation itself obviously does not (Gen. 1:26–28). Male and female equally and complimentarily bear the image of God. Thus women deserve full and total equality in the church and in society because of creation. What about practicing homosexuals within the church?

Civil society may, of course, determine, as a matter of human rights, that both homosexuals and heterosexuals deserve equal rights in every respect, as is happening now in the United States. But the Church of Jesus Christ necessarily adheres to a higher moral standard because of its covenant relationship to God through Jesus Christ. If the church betrays that higher standard in one area (for example, social justice or the treatment of women), that still does not justify nullifying biblical morality in the area of sexuality.

Here again we see that women's rights and the acceptance of homosexual practice are quite different issues. Full equality of women affirms creation and biblical authority. In parallel fashion, the ban on homo-sexual practice as acceptable Christian behavior affirms creation (and recognition of the Fall) and thus affirms biblical authority.

We hasten to add, however, that the biblical command to love is a higher-level truth and ethic than the prohibition of homosexual practice. The proper way to reconcile these is conceptually clear, though difficult in practice: Christians must show unbounded love toward homo-sexual persons, while not accepting homosexual practice as acceptable in the context of Christian holiness and discipleship. This is consistent with the example of Jesus that we examined at the beginning of the book.

Is this the same as saying, "Hate the sin; love the sinner"? Yes and no. Jesus made it crystal clear that his followers should, at times, hang around and eat with sinners and social outcasts, as he did. We often need to remind ourselves that homosexual sin in itself is no greater than heterosexual sin.

Here the biblical witness is decisive. The unwavering biblical ban on homosexual practice with greater freedom for slaves and women leaves us with an argument that is unanswerable without compromising biblical authority. (I will say more about this later.)

2. The Issue of Family Life

Other important reasons underscore the insistence that homosexuality is a key issue for Christians, beginning with the matter of family stability.

Can a society that condones homosexual practice and homosexual families be stable over time? Perhaps, though it's never been tried in human history.

Christians believe that the *health* of family life and of society over generations depends on continuing to view homosexual behavior as morally offensive from a Christian standpoint, even if it is accepted in society.

God's plan as revealed in Scripture has to do with families, and with maintaining covenant fidelity over generations. (Note the biblical emphasis on "generations," which I discuss in *Salvation Means Creation Healed.*[6])

Healthy society, and certainly healthy church life, depends on healthy family life. The church is the family of God and the Christian family is the church of God.

True, Jesus did not base his initial community of disciples on biological family units. Christian brotherhood and sisterhood transcends biological brotherhood and sisterhood. Yet, the Bible and the Christian gospel clearly teach that the biological family unit (male and female united and normally procreative) is foundational in God's plan and in the formation and generational fidelity of His people. "For this reason a man shall leave his father and mother and be joined to his wife, and the two shall become one flesh" (Matt. 19:5; cf. Gen. 2:24).

Consider the many biblical injunctions to "teach your children" the ways of the Lord (for example, Deut. 11:19). This implies two things: that men and women will, in most cases, wed and have children and that they are to teach them what the Bible says about sexual and gender relationships. If these two things are not done, obviously society will drift from God's ways.

The church is based largely (though not exclusively) on marriage and family life, and stable, healthy society is built largely on healthy and stable Christian families. Maintaining biblical standards of sexual and gender relationships contributes to social stability over generations.

We have entered a time, especially in the West, when same-sex couples are marrying and raising either adopted or biological children—that is, children of one or the other or both parties in the same-sex union by using surrogate partners. Whether such families can be stable over generations remains to be seen. Perhaps so, and perhaps as much as heterosexual unions, which of course, often are dysfunctional and/or end in divorce. But even if such family arrangements prove to be stable over generations, they will model a morality, at least with regard to sexuality, that is contrary to biblical teachings.[7] The revealed biblical pattern is the wiser and healthier way.

3. The Image of God

"God created humankind in his image, in the image of God he created them" (Gen. 1:27). Man and woman were created in full equality, with a commission to jointly and compassionately "rule" and steward the earth.

Human creation in God's image is a hugely important fact, practically and theologically, as John Wesley recognized so profoundly. It has essential implications for salvation, holiness, and new creation. And it speaks to the issue of homosexuality.

Human creation as male and female is in some sense a reflection of the unity and diversity of the Holy Trinity. When the Tri-Personal God creates, gendered humankind is the result. The profound unity-in-diversity of the Trinity is in a derivative sense reflected in the unity-in-diversity of the human family—mother, father, offspring. God is beyond and yet in some sense incorporates gender. In creation, the richness of Triune life produces gender distinction within the unity of human personhood.

In other words, the distinction between male and female, and the complementarity they share, is built into creation. Its source is the unity of and distinction between the Persons of the Trinity.

This fact does not resolve all issues regarding homosexuality (as some Christians may be tempted to think). However it does weigh on the side of biblical morality, with its prohibition of homosexual practice, since the obvious implication of male-female distinction is male-female union in marriage. This is assumed throughout the Bible.

Gendered human creation in the image of God is a core matter of human identity. Clearly it establishes the biblical norm for persons, families, societies, and culture. It is basic to the biblical covenants. The sexual ethic of Scripture (both hetero and homo) is an integral and coherent part of the biblically revealed plan of salvation.

Since salvation means creation healed, salvation in its fullness will always mean healing also in this area of gender relationships—short-term, and/or long-term, in the fullness of God's plan and purposes.

In all that follows, this central fact of human creation in the divine image is an underlying theme.

4. Countercultural Identity and Witness

As it seeks to follow God's ways, the church will always be countercultural at key points. Those points vary over time and according to cultural context. Today, an essential mark of countercultural identity and witness concerns homosexuality.

There is no point in being countercultural just to be "counter" or different (which the church sometimes forgets). In every context the church is in some aspects

cultural, in others *subcultural*, and in still others *countercultural*. The key question is always: What does fidelity to
Jesus Christ and God's covenant and kingdom mean *here
and now*, in current society?

Today—in the West, but increasingly globally
—homosexuality is a key and strategic issue of countercultural identity and witness. It is not the only one,
nor even the most important. Today's church needs to
be countercultural in caring for the earth; in ministering
with and among the poor; in building loving community
in the face of individualism and personal isolation; in its
rejection of materialism, consumerism, and commodification; in redeeming the arts and economics. It should
be countercultural in standing against materialism,
consumerism, and commodification (that is, putting a
price tag on everything), as well as other areas. But for all
the reasons cited, homosexuality is a key area of countercultural witness.

The issue here is not primarily negative: condemna-
tion. Rather, it is positive: embodying and incarnating a
better, more healthful, more fulfilling and generationally
sustainable way of life. A better way. Faithful Christian
community models a healthier path as it really demonstrates the love of Jesus Christ.

Gender relationships are a key area where Christians
can give powerful, positive witness—not so much through
what we say or condemn, but by what we show in our

own lives and loves. This happens through embodying the biblical covenant in believers' relationships with God, with the earth, and with one another, whether in marriage or singleness.

These four points closely intertwine—scriptural witness, family life, the image of God, and counter-cultural identity. They lay a biblical and theological foundation. With that foundation in place, we can go on to look at specific questions and biblical passages that deal with sexual morality.

On the Other Hand!

So the argument here is at heart positive, not negative. Healthy, pure, licit gender relationships are one of the great blessings of living God's way. This includes the blessing of Christian friendships among men and women. Very close but nonerotic friendships, both cross-gender and same-sex, are a wonderful benefit of the gospel. Jesus' own life shows this beautifully, as does the witness of the early church. Biblically, human relationships are rich, varied, multidimensional—much wider and broader and more beautiful than relationships based solely or primarily on sex.

But wait. We need to add some qualifications and clarifications, because the issues here are complex.

As Christians, we are called to extend compassion and understanding in the area of sexual relations just as much as in others. Just as Jesus did. We should go as far as Christian truth and Jesus' example will allow in accepting homosexuals.

Christian doctrine rests on love and truth. Love without truth is not true love. Truth without love undermines itself; it becomes untruth. We seek to demonstrate God's love in the fullest, truest ways without compromising biblical truth. In this connection, I commend the approach of Thomas Hopko in his insightful little book *Christian Faith and Same-Sex Attraction: Eastern Orthodox Reflections*.

Hopko, former dean of St. Vladimir's Seminary, says Christians should view same-sex attraction from a revealed biblical perspective, regardless of how countercultural that is—even as we learn also from ongoing social-scientific studies. He writes, "[H]aving loving desires for people of one's own sex is not at all sinful; it is perfectly natural, normal, and necessary."[8] When such desires are erotic or lead to homosexual behavior, however, they are sinful and must be dealt with as such— compassionately, understandingly, firmly. (Here Hopko draws on C. S. Lewis.)

Hopko views erotic same-sex attraction through the lens of discipleship. All Christians are cross bearers. Christians struggling with homosexual tendencies, whatever their source, are no different except in the nature of their struggle. They should "see their refusal to act out their feelings sexually as an extraordinary opportunity for imitating Christ" rather than conforming to the world.[9]

We must not minimize the struggle, however. A Christian friend recently described to me the pain and confusion of growing up with homosexual desires. "Imagine what it is like for a kid to grow up with same-sex attraction and never feel like there was a safe place to talk about it. I was a person who felt trapped, ashamed, and who didn't want to let people down.

So understanding, compassion, and openness are essential. But that is not the same as approving or endorsing the behavior.

Hopko rightly insists therefore that Christians must love homosexuals. We should defend their civil rights, including domestic partnerships. "Civil unions" are not Christian marriage but can provide necessary protections in our fallen world. They are important especially for children growing up in families based on same-sex unions. We must recognize that civil and multi-religious society is not the Church of Jesus Christ—a key distinction.

[Section Two]

Core Issue versus Essential Doctrine

I stated in Section One that homosexual behavior is a core issue for Christian faith and witness because it involves fundamental issues of Christian doctrine. I do not mean (as some readers of the original *Seedbed* post assumed) that the prohibition of homosexual practice is itself an essential doctrine. Not at all.

By *core issue* I mean that one's position on homosexual practice involves a set of assumptions about biblical authority and salvation that are critical to Christian faith and practice. The integrity of our faith is at stake, in both doctrine and behavior (which are, at heart, one). That is the thesis that underlies the four points discussed in Section One.

The biblical ban on homosexual practice is not itself an essential doctrine. This is true for two reasons. First, neither the Bible nor the church's historic creeds deal directly with this question. Second, biblical teachings on salvation, and specifically on justification by faith, ground salvation in God's grace, not our behavior.

But this does not lessen the seriousness of the issue. The logic of the ban on homosexual practice in both the Old and the New Testaments makes it clear that this prohibition is a *necessary implication* of the call to holiness (as I discuss more fully in Section Three).

Notice Paul's reasoning in Romans 1:18–32. Whatever the details of interpretation, the central argument is clear. It takes a twisted logic to simply cut out or explain away the denunciation of homosexual behavior here. The alternative, of course—if one does not like what Paul says—is to argue that Paul got it wrong. So we simply dismiss this passage. Today many folks take this path, using various forms of logic and interpretation to prove the passage is really irrelevant or means something different from what it says.

Perhaps Paul overreacts here? Speaks contrary to the spirit of Jesus? No. That contradicts sound biblical interpretation. As John Nolland notes, arguments mounted against the relevance and plain sense of Romans 1 have "not been found persuasive by very many biblical scholars who have worked closely on Romans."[1]

In fact, Paul's argument in Romans 1 underscores the importance and relevance of Romans 6:1–14. "Should we continue in sin in order that grace may abound? By no means! How can we who died to sin go on living in it?" Having been "baptized into Christ Jesus," we are to "walk in newness of life. . . . We know that our old self was crucified with him so that the body of sin might be destroyed, and we might no longer be enslaved to sin. . . . Therefore, do not let sin exercise dominion in your mortal bodies, to make you obey their passions. No longer present your members to sin as instruments [or weapons] of wickedness, but present yourselves to God as those who have been brought from death to life, and present your members to God as instruments [or weapons] of righteousness. For sin will have no dominion over you, since you are not under law but under grace."

There is no basis in Paul or anywhere else in Scripture to claim that this passage refers to all other forms of biblically banned behavior, but not to homosexual behavior. Romans 6:1–14 speaks very pointedly to all of us, all who are determined to follow Jesus Christ faithfully at whatever cost. No special exemptions for special identities or preferences or proclivities of whatever sort.

I won't take time here to list or discuss all the Bible texts that deal with homosexual practice. That has been done repeatedly by many authors.[2] Virtually all those who accept the full authority of Scripture and the historical facts of God's work of salvation in Jesus Christ come to essentially the same conclusion. John Stott gives a concise summary of the historic consensus in his comments on Romans 1, as follows:

> God created humankind male and female; God instituted marriage as a heterosexual union; and what God has thus united, we have no liberty to separate. This threefold action of God established that the only context which he intended for the "one flesh" experience is heterosexual monogamy, and that a homosexual partnership (however loving and committed it may claim to be) is "against nature" and can never be considered as a legitimate alternative to marriage.[3]

Today many disagree with this historic consensus. They raise a mountain of objections in order to affirm some forms of homosexual behavior as acceptable for Christians. I find these arguments irreconcilable with both Scripture and the logic of salvation through Jesus Christ. The fundamental issue, it turns out, is not really biblical interpretation, but biblical authority. Not hermeneutics, but obedience.

In sum: the question of homosexual practice is not in itself a matter of essential Christian doctrine. But one cannot condone homosexual practice without running into conflict with—and thus in practice disregarding—essential Christian doctrine and the authority of God's Word.

A Biblical Case Study

Raise the question of biblical authority, and Christians who condone homosexual practice have an answer: the biblical evidence is slight or ambiguous. Or involves disputed exegesis. True?

A good way to answer is indirectly, through examining several biblical passages. So, let's do a biblical case study, selecting two related texts from the Old Testament and two from the New, and see what we can learn.

Old Testament Example

From the Old Testament, let's compare Leviticus 18:22 and Deuteronomy 22:5:

You shall not lie with a male as with a woman; it is an abomination (Lev. 18:22).

A woman shall not wear a man's apparel, nor shall a man put on a woman's garment; for whoever does such things is abhorrent to the LORD your God (Deut. 22:5).

These two passages are quite similar. Yet the church recognizes the second prohibition as no longer applicable. Why not the first also, which in its obvious meaning refers to homosexual behavior? (Note that Leviticus 18:22 says nothing about homosexual *tendencies* or *desire* or *orientation*. In fact, this and similar passages implicitly assume that some males will desire such behavior or have such attraction.)

First let's note the similarities in these two biblical commands. Both involve gender. Both speak of behavior that is "abhorrent" or "abominable" to God. Is there a key difference? Why not let both restrictions sleep quietly in the musty pages of the Old Testament rather than dragging them forward as issues of behavior for Jesus-followers today?

Two key reasons.

1. The first reason is the point made by William Webb, discussed earlier. While we can clearly trace redemptive movement in Scripture on a good many issues, including

the rights of women and slaves, *we find no such movement with regard to issues of sexual behavior* (specifically homosexual behavior, in this case). In contrast, there clearly is redemptive movement with regard to food and apparel as we move from the Old to the New Covenant. (See for example 1 Corinthians 10:23–33 and Jesus' teaching and example in Mark 7:14–19.)

As a matter of fundamental biblical interpretation, I believe this point is decisive with regard to homosexual behavior—as it is with regard to heterosexual behavioral purity. The command stands as forcefully at the end of the Bible as it does earlier.

2. A second key point: *the ban on homosexual behavior is based on the moral law, not the ceremonial law.* It deals with a much more fundamental issue of moral identity and behavior than does banning certain clothing.

The relation between the moral law and the ceremonial law is a complex issue. Whole books have been written on it. Historically, much of the debate has concerned marriage and divorce and Sabbath observance, though food and clothing have also gotten their share of attention through the ages.

We needn't go into those debates. The point is that the general Christian consensus throughout history holds that the ceremonial law ended with the coming of Jesus, who embodies and fulfills the law and its intended purpose. The moral law, on the other hand, continues because it is based in God's character, which in turn is reflected in creation and the Ten Commandments. Confining sexual relations to the marriage union between a man and a woman and banning homosexual behavior both express the moral law, not the ceremonial law.

To put it better: biblical teachings regarding sexual relations reflect *who God is* in his personhood, character, and holiness. This is true actually for all the relations we have with each other and with God's other creatures and the whole world of nature.

Both the moral law and the ceremonial law reflect God's character. But whereas the ceremonial law was given for a specific stage in salvation history, the moral law holds for all time. It transcends all cultures and epochs of human history since it reveals the very character of God and, correspondingly, reflects the deep abiding truth of human creation in the image of God.

This is consistenet with Jesus' teaching. Discussing marriage and divorce, Jesus goes back to the "in the beginning" state of things. (For instance, Mark 10:6, "From the beginning of creation, 'God made them male and female.'") It is worth noting that Jesus says *nothing* about clothing or "cross-dressing," which are not grounded in creation. Adam and Eve "were both naked, and were not ashamed" (Gen. 2:25). But that was before sin entered. (Interestingly, the text doesn't say whether the clothing God later provided them was gender-specific! See Genesis 3:21.)

Many Mosaic covenant restrictions no longer apply now, in the New Covenant in Jesus Christ. Both Jesus and Paul reflected this in their teachings. Those restrictions, however, that are more fundamentally based in creation—and thus grounded more directly in the very character of God and his image in humankind—are for all time and cultures. They are not annulled in the New Covenant. Rather, they are deepened and made a matter of the heart, not merely of behavior.

The best example here is the Sermon on the Mount and Jesus' radical claim, "Do not think that I have come to abolish the law or the prophets; I have come not to abolish but to fulfill" (Matt. 5:17).

As with the Head, so with the Body, the church. "Fulfilling the law" today in our union with Jesus Christ means honoring God and living a life of holiness in all areas (the principle). So regarding dress, gender-specific clothing is no longer required as it was in the OT holiness code. Similarly, "fulfilling the law" now means honoring God and living a life of holiness in all our human interactions, including sexual ones. Since the ban of homosexual behavior is grounded implicitly in creation, and since nothing in the New Testament suggests otherwise, we have no biblical permission to say that the Old Testament prohibitions of homosexual behavior no longer apply.

But what about New Testament teachings? Christians regularly ignore some of its behavioral restrictions. Is this justifiable? Let's see.

New Testament Example

Consider Romans 1:26–32 and 1 Corinthians 11:4–10:

> For this reason God gave them up to degrading passions. Their women exchanged natural intercourse for unnatural, and in the same way also the men, giving up natural intercourse with women, were consumed with passion for one another. Men committed shameless acts with men and received in their own persons the due penalty for their error. . . . They know God's decree, that those who practice such things deserve to die—yet they not only do them but even applaud others who practice them (Rom. 1:26–27, 32).

> Any man who prays or prophesies with something on his head disgraces his head, but any woman who prays or prophesies with her head unveiled disgraces her head—it is one and the same thing as having her head shaved. . . . For this reason a woman ought to have a symbol of authority on her head, because of the angels (1 Cor. 11:4–5, 10).

Today, most Christians hold that the second prohibition no longer applies. Why not the first, which in its obvious meaning bans homosexual behavior?

The two passages are similar. Both involve gender issues. Both speak of behavior that is prohibited. Is there a key difference? If issues of head covering are now irrelevant, why not also the ban on homosexual behavior?

Two crucial responses:

1. These prohibitions actually *confirm William Webb's point about redemptive movement.* The New Covenant gospel provides much more freedom of expression for women in the Christian community than we find in Old Testament Israel. The gospel brings more liberty, less restrictions, for now Christ has come and the gospel is offered without price to the nations, irrespective of culture.

The culturally diverse context of the early church is a big part of the picture here. Jewish law no longer applies. What remain, however, are practical guidelines for how godly men and women (now including Gentiles) are to behave within first-century Greco-Roman society.

This guidance is what Paul provided. Redemptive movement is seen here in Christian women's greater freedom. This, in turn, calls for some practical, culturally specific guidelines—which Paul supplies, but which may not apply in other times and contexts, or perhaps not in the same way.

In contrast, we find no softening or lessening of the ban on homosexual behavior.

2. *The second response relates even more to the cultural context.* John Nolland noted correctly that in 1 Corinthians 11 "the appeal to nature is nothing more than an appeal to culture."[1] The situation of the early church was hugely different from (though not unrelated to) the situation of Israel under the Mosaic covenant, discussed above. Culture and cultural context come into play in a much more decisive way now that God's people are not defined primarily by their relationship to Abraham and Moses, but by their relationship to Jesus Christ, who opens the door of salvation to all people of all races and cultures—the door of salvation and the call to holiness.

The key difference between Old and New Testament teachings about clothing is that the Old Testament prohibitions are based on ceremonial holiness, while the New Testament restrictions are based on gospel contextualization. All these teachings, however, both on clothing and on homosexuality, concern what it means to lead a holy, wholesome life before God and in relation to others within the larger plan of God.

In 1 Corinthians 11, Paul shows how Christian men and women should express their new radical freedom in Christ in their place and time—specifically, Corinth, in this case. He summarizes the common Jewish understanding about what is appropriate in hair and head coverings. But then he makes a radical break in verses 11–12: "Nevertheless, *in the Lord* woman is not independent of man or man independent of woman. For just as woman came from man, so man comes through woman; but all things come from God."

Paul's argument here: *in the Lord* there is no distinction (as he says elsewhere, for example in Galatians 3:28). There is full freedom and equality in Christ, and thus in the body of Christ. But *in the present cultural context*, Paul says, you should practice some common-sense restrictions in order not to give offense.

Though not stated, the implied assumption here is that the radical freedom both women and men enjoy in Christ will more and more leaven society all around. This is in fact the role of the body of Christ in culture. This is our transforming mission: to shine forth the gospel in society and to make disciples in all nations and ethnicities in ways consistent with God's revealed character.

Precisely here we find the difference with regard to homosexual behavior. The logic of Romans 1 is not that homosexual behavior should be banned so as not to give offense (as with head coverings), or as a temporary measure. Rather it is that homosexual behavior is contrary to God's moral law, given for all time, reflecting God's unchanging character. There is thus a finality to it that stands above any and all societies.

Examining these Old and New Testament passages, we see that at every level the Bible consistently teaches a moral ethic that excludes homosexual behavior from acceptance by Christians.

There is another option, of course: to regard the Bible's teaching as not authoritative on this issue. If pro-homosexual arguments can't be sustained by any sound principles of biblical interpretation, only one option remains: admit that the Bible really does ban homosexual behavior, but decide that the Bible is not the final authority here.

Today many follow this path. But Christians who take the Bible, faithfully interpreted through the lens of Jesus Christ, as final authority, won't follow this road. Homosexuality is not as important or as central as, say, the incarnation and resurrection of Jesus Christ. But ultimately the same issue is at stake: the authority of Scripture. If we deny or disregard the biblical witness on homosexuality, we put some other authority above Scripture. In most cases, this higher authority is our own reasoning. (This is discussed further in Section Five.)

Holy Homosexuals?

Can people in committed same-sex relationships at the same time be faithful Christian disciples? Today many Christians, homosexual and heterosexual alike, claim they can. Committed same-sex relationships and Christian discipleship are not incompatible, according to this view.

I contest this, and here's why.

Holy Living Does Not Equal Doctrinal Correctness

We should note first, however, that a devout and holy life is not the same as doctrinal fidelity. Neither does a holy life guarantee ethical consistency. A person may be pure and holy according to their conscience and all the light they have, but may still have unrecognized areas of ethical inconsistency and faulty doctrine in their lives. Many saints (and those of us who aspire to be saints) were and are well aware of this. Saints can be holy and still quirky. So also with many "ordinary" Christians.

Consider some examples.

A Christian slaveholder in the 1700s lived a devout and holy life. He treated his slaves well, as admonished in the New Testament. His sincere holy life was consistent except for this one glaring injustice of slavery (which, in fact, he justified biblically).

Another example: several devout Christians I knew when I was growing up were models of godliness and compassion. Yet they were racists. Their holiness was sincere and true, but not whole. It had not reached through to their racial attitudes.

It's hard to imagine now, but in the 1940s the very godly wife of a Christian college president told a young woman student she shouldn't marry her boyfriend because he was Italian. "We don't believe in interracial marriage, you know," she told the student.

Finally, a contemporary example. Many devout evangelical Christians practice their faith in every area of their life except one: they ignore God's covenant with the earth (Gen. 9) and our responsibility to care for God's good creation.

So also when it comes to homosexuality. A considerable number of sincere, devout Christians follow Jesus and are faithful in many areas—but with the exception of their sexual behavior. I am sure there are devout Christians who live the homosexual "lifestyle." They are sincere. Yet their sincerity and devotion, however genuine, do not justify their homosexual practice any more than evangelical Christians' sincere spirituality justifies their disregard of creation care or their racism.

Further, we can in love confess that a person who fails to care for the earth but has no awareness or consciousness of violating God's Word, and yet is fully trusting in God for salvation through Jesus Christ, can despite this area of unfaithfulness be saved through Christ's atonement. Surely then the same must apply to Christians who are practicing homosexuals, provided they are living with a pure, not a seared, conscience. In both cases: Lord, have mercy.

Whether there really are such persons, of course— and how many—is known only to God. But we should all pray that God will lead us to a fuller grasp of the truth so that we may embody God's will and ways in all areas of our lives.

Someone will say, of course, that creation care and homosexuality are not similar; that homosexual practice is a much greater offense in God's eyes. Perhaps so. Maybe not. However, I don't want to get into the business of ranking sins. In the past that has often led to legalism or hypocrisy. God knows the heart. I think of Jesus' words: "Why do you see the speck in your neighbor's eye, but do not notice the log in your own eye?" (Matt. 7:3).

Homosexuals: "Born that way"?

Today many people suspect that homosexuality has a genetic base. Some persons are simply "born that way." Or "hard-wired" to be gay. It's not their choice. So surely Christians should accept their homosexuality simply as a legitimate part of their humanity. In the case of Christians, their homosexual behavior should be accepted as compatible with their Christian faith.

There are several responses to this, and a growing literature. I make just three points.

First, *no genetic basis for homosexuality has as yet been established*. The jury is out. A number of people who have studied the matter see no credible evidence of a genetic basis for homosexual tendencies or behavior. On the other hand, same-sex attraction clearly shows up very early in some children, raising the question of whether it is inborn.

Today issues of homosexuality get a huge amount of media attention, but that very fact can distort perceptions. Most research shows that only a small percentage of people consider themselves to be homosexuals or report same-sex sexual contact. One study in 2006 in which people responded anonymously found that while 20 percent had experienced homosexual feelings, only 2 to 3 percent considered themselves to be homosexuals.

John Stott's summary of the evidence is useful:

> [Research so far suggests] that in the Western world, putting aside teenage experimentation, between 3% and 5.5% of men have undertaken a homosexual act in their adult lifetime, between 1.5% and 4% of men have had a homosexual partner in the last five years, and less than 2% of the male population, and less than 1% of the female, are exclusively homosexual in inclination and practice.[1]

The point here, however, is not the state of the research but simply that the question of a genetic basis for homosexuality remains open and much disputed.

Second, *even if a genetic basis were to be found, that would not change the ethical question for Christians*. We are all affected by the Fall. We all have inborn tendencies to follow our own way, not God's.

Consider this: Some people and ethnic groups have a particular susceptibility to alcoholism due to their genetic makeup. Should we therefore consider alcoholism normal and acceptable for them?

No, because we know the bondage that alcoholism brings. We will have special compassion for such people.

We will express that compassion by doing what we can to prevent alcoholism, especially among people we love and know.

So also with homosexuality. Should it ever be established that some people are "born that way," we will have compassion for them and help them deal with this proclivity in ways consistent with the gospel.

In other words, inborn tendencies, where they exist, do not justify indulging those tendencies in sinful or destructive ways. We seem clearly to understand this in other areas; there is no reason to make an exception in the case of homosexuality.

Third, we need to recognize that *social trends, cultural context, and particular experiences can lead heterosexual persons into homosexual behavior.*

John Wenham, a British evangelical leader who died in 1996, made an interesting comment in his remarkably candid autobiography, *Facing Hell.* Wenham describes his adolescent sexual awakening. "I remember a stage when I was distinctly attracted to a good-looking senior boy. I can understand the danger of a boy's sexual orientation becoming distorted if he is encouraged to think of himself as homosexual at this stage and is not allowed to grow through it naturally. Fortunately for me this problem did not arise and my prayer for needed knowledge [about sex] was answered."[2]

Just so. That was back in the 1920s. Think how much more timely this insight is today. We could add to Wenham's comment about "sexual orientation becoming distorted": especially if one is prompted to think of oneself as homosexual, or if a teen or preteen has no sexual instruction or is encouraged to explore different sexual "options."

Recently I was talking with a friend of mine, a woman who is a United Methodist pastor. She has several lesbian friends. As a pastor, she has counseled women dealing with same-sex attraction.

My friend startled me with this comment: "Some lesbians are very aggressive in recruiting others," she said. A young woman may be told, "Just try it and see."

One wonders how many unsuspecting young men and women, girls and boys, are led into homosexuality who in other contexts would have grown into healthy heterosexual identities.

Certainly in some cases genetic factors play a role in same-sex attraction and orientation. But no doubt in many cases—perhaps the majority—one's own life experiences play a key, and not always healthy, role.

In other words, genetics is not destiny. Thankfully. Whoever we are, we are morally responsible, with moral choices. That applies as much to homosexuality as it does to any other dynamic in our life and being.

I will not enter here into the controversy as to whether homosexuals "can change"—that is, become heterosexuals—and if so to what degree, how permanently, and by what means. I do however recommend *Ex-gays? A Longitudinal Study of Religiously Mediated Change in Sexual Orientation*[3], by Stanton Jones and Mark Yarhouse. Their careful and nuanced study found that "change of homosexual orientation may be possible" in some cases. Their findings "appear to contradict the commonly expressed view of the mental health establishment that change of sexual orientation is impossible and that the attempt to change is highly likely to produce harm for those who make such an attempt."[4]

Personal accounts suggest that at least in some cases, homosexuals can change, deeply. Consider the remarkable testimony of Rosaria Butterfield. Rosaria movingly describes her "train wreck conversion," as she calls it.

Rosaria was a professor of English and women's studies with a keen concern for "morality, justice, and compassion," she says. She was happy being "a leftist lesbian professor" in a respected university. "My partner and I shared many vital interests," including social justice activism.

An article Rosaria wrote attacking "the unholy trinity of Jesus, Republican politics, and patriarchy" generated lots of fan mail, but also hate mail. One letter, however, didn't fit either category. It troubled her, because the writer kindly and courteously asked her to examine her own presuppositions and assumptions, as any good academic should.

She eventually met this writer, who turned out to be a gentle Presbyterian pastor. Rosaria had dinner with him and his wife, and they became friends. Soon Rosaria started reading the Bible. "I read the way a glutton devours." This opened into a chain of events that eventually led to a personal faith in Christ and turned her world upside down—"a train wreck." She writes, "I weakly believed that if Jesus could conquer death, he could make right my world. I drank, tentatively at first, then passionately, of the solace of the Holy Spirit. I rested in private peace, then community, and today in the shelter of a covenant family, where one calls me 'wife' and many call me 'mother.'"[5]

It would be misleading to hold up Rosaria's experience as typical. People's characters and stories vary widely. As with alcoholism and other issues, some Christians may struggle all their lives, yet others find immediate or perhaps gradual deliverance.

Whatever the situation or circumstances that lead a person into homosexual behavior, God's grace is sufficient, for it is made perfect in our weakness (2 Cor. 12:9).

Accommodation Theology

Some sincere Christians struggling with the homosexuality issue have found a haven in what is called "accommodation theology." Historically the term "accommodation" has been used to speak of the way God "accommodates" or adapts himself to human and cultural limitations in order for his self-revelation to be understood. The *Oxford Dictionary of the Christian Church* defines accommodation as "the adaptation of a text or teaching to altered circumstances."[6] The term has been used in various ways, including "the modification of the form of Christian teaching to secure its more ready acceptance."[7]

Applied to current debates over homosexuality, the idea is that God permits homosexual practice among committed Christians as acceptable, though not his original intent. William Stacy Johnson in *A Time to Embrace* puts it this way: though committed same-sex relationships "are disobedient in form, they may nevertheless be obedient in substance. That is, there may be many virtuous aspects of such relationships even though they depart from the perfect will of God."[8]

One author, Frank Tapper, summarizes accommodationism this way:

Although homosexuality does not fulfill the normative purpose of God in creation for human personhood, homosexuality is an unintended given in emergence of human life in the world. Using the criteria for human personhood in Genesis 2–3, [this view holds that] homosexuality occurred in the creative working of God as an unwanted given that diverged from God's intention in creation. A person who is constitutionally homosexual exhibits the disordering of God's purpose in creation and ought to live out his or her life in a responsible fashion. Thus a gay or lesbian person exists through the creativity of God, but he or she is a recognizable "alteration" and not a perverse "deviation" from the life-giving work of God.[9]

A friend of mine who accepts this view describes accommodation theology as

a non-affirming position that basically says that gay covenant relationships are not God's ideal and are sinful, but they are morally permissible because they are the most moral life available for most people who are gay. I personally believe that gay relationships are celebrated by God. But I appreciate accommodation theology because it honors the humanity of people who are gay, whereas traditionalist theology diminishes that humanity. Accommodation theology provides traditionalists with a way to believe that causes less harm.

Tapper describes this view as neither "welcoming but not affirming" nor "welcoming and celebrating." Rather it is "welcoming and accepting," as an accommodation to human fallenness. A "tragic element" is inescapable here because homosexuality "cannot fulfill the intention of God in the marriage of male and female into oneness or the blessing of child-bearing." Thus "gay and lesbian persons experience the tragic inalterably in the definition of their sexual identity" and often especially in their relationship with other Christians.[10]

So this is a compromise position—really an accommodation.

I can accept this to a point. I appreciate the sincerity and intent of those who view "accommodation" as an option. Truly they want and intend to be faithful Christians. Theologically it is not a real solution, however, because it stretches the principle of accommodation to human fallenness to the point of denying biblical teaching that is grounded in something deeper than cultural context. In effect it makes fallible human reasoning higher than biblical authority.

Of course Christians who believe that God fully accepts and celebrates committed same-sex unions would reject accommodationism out of hand, since it makes practicing homosexuals second-class citizens in the church.

Joy in Obedience

People are always better off obeying God's Word than dismissing or fudging it. This certainly is as true regarding homosexuality as it is in other areas. Obedience to God's Word brings joy, fulfillment, and healthy community.

Am I suggesting, then, that people with homosexual desires will be happier, more content, less conflicted, and more fulfilled if as a spiritual discipline they refrain from homosexual behavior?

Yes, definitely!

Christian history offers us a rich tapestry of people finding much greater fulfillment in self-denial for the sake of holiness and mission than in unfettered self-expression. True, that sounds hollow, even hypocritical, when one is recommending self-denial to someone else. But clearly the fundamental truth applies to everyone, irrespective of the issue, including matters of gender and sexual expression.

I know there are people whose body is the opposite of their emotional makeup—folks who are, shall we say, male on the outside but female on the inside, or vice versa. Such persons can experience enormous conflict and anguish. Here the body of Christ must open its arms with understanding, acceptance, counsel, and healing community.

These people are not responsible for their dilemma. Probably it is impossible to know why this is so in a particular person. How much is genetics (or genetic mutation), early childhood formation, or some other dynamic involved?

Percentagewise, such individuals are very few. But that only makes their anguish greater and their difference more marked. Probably there has always been a small minority of such folks.[11] Their presence and dilemma become much more pronounced, however, in a society that is sex-permeated, sex-exploited, sexually confused, and socially networked at the peer level, as is increasingly true now. This is an important missional challenge for today's church.

What happens when you live in a society where sex is so commercialized and exploited as it is today? When sex is used to sell everything from cars to toothpaste?

Several things. Every issue and topic acquires an underlying sexual subtext or tone that is nearly unavoidable. A below-the-surface latent energy. People come to believe that personal meaning and fulfillment are bound up essentially or primarily with sexual experience. (Untrue.)

This is a problem for everyone. For many, this assumption is part of their unquestioned worldview. This sex-absorbed myth is especially problematic and poisonous for young folks and/or for people who already struggle with issues of gender identity. Even more so in a society that is highly individualistic, commercialized, and peer-networked rather than being networked through cross-generational family ties.

But this is where we are today. Result: people seek meaning and fulfillment in sex (in one form or another) rather than in healthy community where men, women, and children interact with one another in many dimensions, not just sexual ones.

For lots of people, the real problem is not sex but the loss of healthy community. Without healthful, holistic community, people seek meaning and fulfillment in a spectrum of individualistic and often self-destructive ways.

How does such a social context affect people who experience gender confusion or conflict, or people who feel same-sex attraction? Often such folks are led (or persuaded, or seduced) to believe their happiness lies in full and unrestricted expression of their sexual desires, rather than in integrating sex into a much broader range of fulfilling life experiences.

[Section Five]

Questions, Answers, More Questions

The preceding discussion, of course, leaves many questions unanswered. I haven't engaged all the issues homosexual practice raises for Christians. The case presented here in fact touches off an explosion of questions, comments, and objections.

Many such reactions and questions have already come my way. Here is an assortment of responses I received to my *Seedbed* posts and from early readers of the book. Perhaps my answers will help clear up some points of confusion, or at least clarify areas of disagreement. (I use pseudonyms to preserve confidentiality and have condensed some of the longer comments.)

Fred: I must disagree. First off in all your education you missed something glaringly obvious. Homosexuality is not a "feeling" that can or should be "borne like a cross." It's not a disorder or disease. For centuries people like you have picked our Scriptures apart and used them to separate us and alienate those that need to hear the words of our Lord Jesus.

The "core issue" is that we continue to alienate and offend our brothers and sisters, only separating them more from the love of Christ. Now who is the real sinner here? You should be ashamed of yourself.

Response: Fred, I agree fully with your concern. I never said or hinted that homosexuality itself is a "feeling," though I do refer to sexual *desire*, whether homosexual or heterosexual, and to same-sex attraction.

Of course, homosexuality involves much more than feelings. Yet heterosexuals as well as homosexuals do experience erotic feelings toward people they find attractive. That's how we're made.

But certainly we recognize that not everything we feel should be accepted or given in to. We have minds and wills as well as emotions. Homosexuality is very complex because personhood is complex. Our sexuality involves every aspect of our being, spiritual as well as mental and physical. Today's culture, however, prioritizes feelings and emotions over will and reason. ("It can't be wrong when it feels so right!")

So I am not ashamed of myself on this point. But I am ashamed when Christians fail fully to show the love of Christ to people with whom they disagree.

Jason: I have long nurtured and maintained relationships with practicing and celibate homosexuals. The issues at an individual level are complicated and there is enough shame to spread thick as peanut butter on warm toast.

However, my experience is that many homosexuals want what we all want. That is for someone to walk with them, love them, and treat them as human beings first. As Christians, we know our job is to pray for God's call to repentance for those sins made yet unaware and for courage to open to his Spirit so that we may be made whole.

Response: Yes! I fully agree. In fact I elaborate some on this elsewhere in the essay. Christians are indeed called "to walk with them, love them, and treat them as human beings."

Leslie: I agree with you that homosexuality is indeed a core issue. However, I find that your four reasons are mere conjectures and inferences rather than based on solid biblical principles. Not that I disagree with them. Rather I hope you can provide us with a sounder foundation than you have given.

Response: Point well taken, with regard to the original post. I did not deal with explicit biblical teachings on this issue, since I assumed they would be well-known.

However, what you call "conjectures and inferences" are really much more than that. Sound theology is based on the whole sweep of Scripture. The ancient church called this *the rule of faith*—in essence, the master story of creation and redemption through Jesus Christ. Any interpretation of specific texts that is out of sync with this rule of faith is a misinterpretation. I believe I show how the specific texts on this matter fit into the master story in a way that yields practical guidance.

Gerald: If homosexuality were a core issue, the Bible should have addressed it much more clearly. Most of the New Testament references are linguistically questionable, and Jesus probably would have mentioned the issue if it is really that important.

Response: First off, the idea that biblical references to homosexuality are ambiguous or unclear or "linguistically questionable" is a popular myth today—but still a myth, as I have shown.

But to your main point: The Bible leaves lots of ethical questions unanswered. Jesus apparently expected us to work these out for ourselves, guided by the Spirit and the Word, in Christian community, in ways consistent with his teachings. On key issues Jesus gave examples—probably ones that were especially relevant to the particular time and place. He could not mention every issue. He expected his followers to know the Old Testament and later to be guided by the New.

If Jesus (and the Bible generally) answered all our questions, this would create three problems. First, the Bible would be five or ten times longer. Second, many teachings would now work cross-culturally, since every moral issue is embedded in culture. The Bible would quickly appear outdated and irrelevant. Third, the church would get so mired in legalism as to lose all openness and vitality.

In other words, if the Bible answered every possible question, the Jesus Movement would never have gotten off the ground. It would have died in Jerusalem or have been stillborn in Antioch.

Frank: I preached on a Sunday morning at the two packed-out services of the local Metropolitan Community Church [which affirms homosexual unions] and have gotten to know the pastor (a Bob

Jones University grad) and members of the congregation through their outstanding service to our city's homeless neighbors. These Christians don't appear to have lost either a sense of biblical authority or earnestness in following in Jesus' footsteps. Their worship and service to others surpasses many who condemn them.

Response: Frank, this is a very important reminder. Christians who do not condone homosexual practice need to appreciate this truth. That's why I discuss the matter elsewhere in this essay. I am thankful for everyone who gives a cup of cold water in Jesus' name.

In the past, some devout holiness people lived godly lives and experienced much of God's presence. They apparently enjoyed the cleansing work of the Spirit in their lives. Yet at the same time some were racists, as I mentioned above. (One hopes this is no longer true.) Genuine, sincere spirituality and sound doctrine do not always go together.

Another point concerning the example you mention: many homosexual Christians experience deep alienation from society, or from other Christians. History shows that people who suffer alienation often have special compassion for other sufferers or victims of society. It rings true therefore that the Metropolitan Community congregation you mention would reach out to help homeless folks. (In his book *Does Jesus Really Love Me?*, Jeff Chu provides interesting insights on the Metropolitan Community Church.)

Marcus: The relational dynamics in my gay and straight friends' marriages seem largely the same. I support Christians not getting all medieval over this issue, but I don't think there's anything to witness over here per se. They're normal people with normal relationships. Christians actually being loving people would go a long ways to keep gays and lesbians from fleeing the churches, though. The sad stories I've heard and read over the years are just heartbreaking.

Response: Point well taken, Marcus. Similar to Frank's comment, I am not interested in condemning or judging anyone in particular, but I am concerned to maintain the integrity of the biblical witness in a spirit of mutual humility and openness.

Rosemary: Has there been much study into what the cultural opinion of homosexuality was in biblical times?

Response: Yes, there is a large and growing literature. William Webb deals with this some in his book *Slaves, Women, and Homosexuals*, and he lists other sources. See also Craig Keener, *The IVP Bible Background*

Commentary: New Testament (Second edition, 2014) on particular passages—for example, Romans 1.

Douglas: The few references to homosexuality in the Bible are as culture-bound as those on women and slavery. One day, God willing, Christians will look back at our present stance on this "core issue" with the same bemused disappointment that we now look back on Rev. George Whitefield's reintroduction of slavery to Georgia on biblical grounds.

Response: Thanks, Douglas. "Few references" is not really accurate, nor is it relevant. When God speaks, once should be enough.

I have, however, pondered the culture argument myself. It is precisely the point Webb examines in his book. Webb shows that in the case of homosexual practice the "culture bound" argument does not hold up according to sound principles of biblical interpretation.

I certainly agree that many of our attitudes on this issue are shaped by culture. That's why my concern is to find a balanced biblical view that is consistent with the life and teachings of Jesus.

Which are more "culture-bound"—biblical teachings on sexual behavior, or today's easy acceptance of homosexual practice? In my view, it's obviously the latter.

Andy: NO, it is not clearly addressed in Romans. The word means effeminate, and if you are making a theology around some obscure passages in Romans and Leviticus, that would not be a convincing theology or ethic.

Response: That would be true, Andy, if this matter really were based on "obscure passages." Throughout the book I show how the matter fits into the flow and logic of the larger biblical revelation.

Andy: The word *homosexual* and the concept of sexual orientation are from the 19th century. Using these terms is like saying the Bible discusses schizophrenia or the cause of disease by virus or bacteria. In a world where slavery exists, men and women both are used as sexual toys by whoever owns them for whatever purpose. We don't execute witches or deny them civil rights. You are entitled and welcome to your belief that you are following the teaching of Jesus. You are not entitled to deny any citizen of the U.S. their civil rights because they offend your religious beliefs. Their religious beliefs and mine stand equal with yours before the Constitution.

Response: Andy, on your last point: Yes, of course. I agree. I make a point above of distinguishing between civil rights and acceptable Christian behavior.

As to your main point—the particular terms we use—you are half right, I think. The words *homosexual* and *homosexuality* are not found in the Bible. Words change over time and pick up various connotations from the cultural context. The Bible does not use the term *environment*, but there is a lot in Scripture about the environment (that is, the created order). Similarly with regard to homosexual practice.

Jim: Howard, my big concern is to make the church a safer place for people who are gay—especially the fourteen-year-old gay kid in the front pew. Really entering into others' pain will lead you to question some of your beliefs about homosexuality and gay Christians if not the traditionalist doctrine itself.

Response: Jim, I admit to still being in learning mode. So thanks. The church should be safe for *everyone*—especially for people like that fourteen-year-old guy or girl.

That is the pressing agenda facing the church. On that we agree, I think. But Jesus himself demonstrates that unlimited compassion does not require compromising the Bible's moral teaching. In fact, just the opposite. Faithfulness to the full biblical revelation, interpreted through Jesus Christ by the Spirit, is the route of true compassion because it leads to redemption. Christians need to understand and practice this as Jesus did.

Julia: Thank you for such clarity of biblical authority. Have you ever interviewed folks who have experienced victory from the homosexual lifestyle into wholeness in Christ? The key was discovering and taking hold of their identity *in Christ*. I could share more with you if you so desire.

Response: No, I have not, though I have heard testimonies. I am sure you are right for it is only in Christ, made real to us through His Spirit and in His Body, that any of us finds wholeness.

Joseph: I think it's worth mentioning that Jesus' lack of explicit mention of homosexuality (though His Matthew 19:12 comments could be taken as such) cannot be taken as some kind of tacit approval. This is an argument from silence that anachronistically imposes a set of contemporary cultural assumptions upon Jesus, and entirely ignores His Jewish context with all its Old Testament legal precedents.

By this logic, one could claim that Jesus "probably would have mentioned" pedophilia, bestiality, polygamy, and incest if He had had any objection to them. Does this make them acceptable? No. This is a gross distortion of the *whole* reading of Scripture and a profoundly dishonest public claim. Paul wrote, "For a time is coming when people will no longer listen to sound and wholesome teaching. They will follow their own desires and will look for teachers who will tell them whatever their itching ears want to hear" (2 Tim. 4:3 NLT).

Response: I see that as an important point in how we interpret the Bible.

Bob: "And the eunuch said to Philip, 'Why can't I be baptized?' And Philip responded, 'Because the Scriptures say that no man who has been emasculated may enter the assembly of the Lord.'" Of course that is not what the text says, but I wonder if you believe it has any relevance to this discussion?

Response: Yes, I think so, in a broad sense. There is expansive new freedom in Christ and thus in relation to Old Testament ceremonial and religious law. This does not, however, negate or relativize the *moral* law, which is more fundamentally based in the holy, loving character of the Triune God.

If the Ethiopian had said instead, "I have a male lover," what would Philip have said? His response likely would have been different because the issue is different.

The prohibition of sexual sins, whether homo or hetero, is clearly not limited to the Old Testament period. The reasons for this are very deep-seated, not based just in individual preference or cultural acceptance. This is what I argue above.

Bob: I wonder whether there is a moral difference between one who is born with a homosexual orientation, for whom same-sex intimacy would be natural and heterosexual intimacy would be unnatural, and the sort of unnatural debauchery referenced in Romans 1. I realize that such a person has the option of remaining celibate, which Paul seems to say is preferential for all of us. But he also seems to concede that celibacy is too much to expect of most Christians.

Response: More work needs to be done, I believe, regarding the dynamics of "homosexual orientation," though a considerable literature does already exist. It will take time and prayer and careful discussion for the church to come to a settled view that is genuinely true and compassionate. It does seem clear that genetic factors do play a role in sexual self-identity, at least for some people.

Marilyn: Homosexuality is a sin, just like all the other ones listed in the Bible: gluttony, lust, greed, etc. When do we put degrees on sin?

Response: Homosexual orientation is not in itself a sin. It can be due to a whole range of factors, many of which are beyond a person's control. If some of these factors are genetic, clearly others are cultural and/or arise from particular family dynamics and from each person's own unique history.

Tony: I'm a gay man. And a Christian. Let me gently say—being gay is at the core of who I am. Not because I'm excessively gay or particularly out there, but because sexuality is a pretty core issue for everyone.

If we are defining ourselves, our humanity, we cannot do so without reference to our sexuality.

I may be a gay man, but please; homosexuality is not a core issue of our faith. That's not because I want to slip my pernicious views into your congregation without you noticing and push unsuspecting elderly down slippery slopes while they aren't looking, it's just because it's true.

Our forebears knew what they were doing when they got hot under the dog collar and wrestled in the theological mud as they worked out the catholic creeds for us. Those creeds aren't a bad place to start looking for what is core. And what do we find?

There are essentials. And there's the rest.

The essentials are about God. The stuff about us (most of it, anyways) comes in the rest. The importance of gendered family structures and necessity of celibate homosexual friendships didn't make it into the catholic creeds. There was a reason. We are not so vital. Try a little humility.

I have a reasonable, worked out biblical take on being gay that doesn't see faithful gay relationships as intrinsically sinful. That's not a majority view, if you read a lot of conservative press, but I don't mind that. I'm a conservative—an evangelical—someone who lives under the Scriptures, and I'm not about to move house. I'm fine with the fact others disagree; of course they do; we disagree on virtually everything else—as long as we all take a moment, breathe, put on our perspective glasses and finally remember what the core issues of our faith actually are.

Response: Tony, I appreciate your candor and honesty. I am sure you have much to teach us.

I agree fully that "sexuality is a pretty core issue for everyone" and we certainly can't define ourselves "without reference to our sexuality." The question is the biblical boundaries within which we are to honor God in the totality of our beings, including our sexuality.

You may indeed have "a reasonable, worked out biblical take on being gay that doesn't see faithful gay relationships as intrinsically sinful." Obviously you mean "reasonable *to me*." But that is not the test. The Bible has much to say about the fallibility of human reason.

One goes against the most obvious, common-sense meaning of Scripture, and against the historic Christian consensus, when one adopts *any* private or personal "reasonable, worked out [allegedly] biblical take" on *any* issue. We need not cite the long list of biblical twistings that were thought by their advocates to be both reasonable and biblical. The Bible itself warns against "one's own interpretation" of the written Word (2 Pet. 1:20–21).

When I was younger I worked out biblical positions (so I thought) on some issues that I now see were plain wrong.

You do, however, make an excellent point about the creeds. I agree fully. They say nothing about homosexuality. They also fail to mention many other important matters. They address issues that were hot topics at the time, and say almost nothing about human behavior as such—or for that matter about the life and teachings of Jesus and what they mean for daily discipleship (as N. T. Wright has emphasized).

Your point seems to imply that I am raising the issue of homosexuality to the status of an essential doctrine. I am not, as I clarify above.

We can say this, however, about the creeds: They are the foundation of much of the Church's Great Tradition, which has seen homosexual practice as wrong and an offense to God. I have argued above that the strong creedal affirmation of the Trinity has important implications for gender relations. But ultimately the basis of our faith is not the creeds but the Word of God revealed to us in Jesus Christ and in Holy Scripture and applied to us and in us by the Holy Spirit.

As to your comment on core identity: I am troubled by the statement, "being gay is at the core of who I am." I would be equally troubled if a Christian said, "being heterosexual is at the core of who I am." What does this mean?

If we are Christians, our identity is in Jesus Christ. That transcends and relativizes *all other* identities, or sources of identity. Sexuality is a core constituent of being human certainly, but whether that sexuality is homo or hetero is often shaped by a multitude of factors, all of which must be handed over unreservedly to Jesus so that we can be formed in His image within His body. Conversion and sanctification are, after all and very fundamentally, a matter of *reorientation*.

In other words, centering our life in Christ— "Christ in us"—deeply reorients everything else in our lives, from sexual self-understanding to worldview and relationships. For most of us, this takes time and discipline and growth and committed participation in Christ's body.

Finally, as to your comment that "the litmus test for understanding whether we have got our measure of God right is the way we treat one another": yes—whether we're talking about sexuality or anything else. We are to treat one another with love, respect, and understanding, including respecting both one's sexuality and God's Word with regard to all our human interactions.

Too often sexual behavior amounts to exploiting and preying on the part of males in relation both to women and to other (most often younger) males. Such behavior is sinful. But really this has less to do with the question of either homosexuality or heterosexuality than it does with the destructive nature of sin itself.

Ward: Natural law arguments like the one you've outlined emphasize the procreative property of sex to the poverty of the unitive property. Sexual promiscuity is not problematic solely because it might lead to pregnancy; promiscuity also carries an emotional toll that potentially harms those who engage in it.

Response: Ward, I agree completely except for your initial suggestion that I am basing my arguments on natural law. I actually don't believe in "natural law" as that term is commonly used. I am attempting to base my understanding on God's self-revelation through Scripture and the created order, but above all on the Living Word, Jesus Christ, who continues to work in our lives by the Spirit.

Yes, the issue is not just procreation but life-giving, mutually nourishing intimacy. The true basis for this is the Triune love of God.

Final Word

I am always reluctant to accept "tipping point" or "slippery slope" arguments. "Domino theories" of events are always shaky; often baseless, overhyped, and with time, proven wrong.

And yet homosexuality is indeed a turning-point issue. It is almost (not quite) a litmus-test issue when it comes to adherence to biblical authority.

For two or three of my respected Evangelical friends, and for a Christian magazine to which I once subscribed, it was exactly that—a very key point. In each case, once homosexual practice was endorsed as acceptable for Christians, other compromises on biblical authority followed. A line had been crossed. The Bible no longer carried the authority it has nearly always had when the church was vital and faithful.

Of course, this is not simple cause-and-effect. Many things can lead to compromises on biblical authority. We wrestle with how faithfully to interpret and apply Scripture across a broad range of issues. But today's popular culture and intellectual climate have pushed homosexuality to the fore in an unprecedented way, making it a critical issue for how we interpret Scripture.

Biblical authority is thus the bigger issue—bigger than the question of homosexuality itself. Biblical fidelity requires viewing homosexual practice as sinful and a violation of God's law. It also requires unfettered compassion and understanding toward homosexual persons in the spirit of Jesus and the sensitivity and power of the Holy Spirit.

In our relationships with *everyone*, including those with same-sex attraction, love comes first, and must come first. We see this in Jesus. His interactions with other people demonstrate that love and acceptance do not mean endorsing homosexual behavior as consistent with the gospel.

Throughout this discussion I have emphasized that faithful Christian behavior means all areas of our lives, not just to homosexuality. There should be no double standard—no pointing the finger or picking specks from others' eyes. But in this book I am focusing specifically on issues of homosexuality in relation to biblical authority.

I recognize that the conversation is not over. The last word has not been said; we all have more to learn and to live into. But if we depart from the church's historic (if sometimes confused) commitment to the authority of God's Word even as we seek better to understand it, we are truly in a moral mess.

One of my best friends in college struggled with sexual identity. I didn't know it at the time. We were both Christians. I knew my friend had deep issues in his Christian walk that he was not able to resolve. In all our many conversations, he never shared with me what those issues were. Yet he was a deeply committed and sincere Christian.

Many years later my friend died of AIDS. I had had only occasional contact with him over the years and knew almost nothing of his personal life. I was shocked when I learned of his illness, and then death. Yet at some level I was not surprised.

I don't know all that happened in my friend's life. Knowing him as I did, however, I am convinced that at some point in his adult life he was sexually exploited—someone taking advantage of his confusion—and led into a life that he knew, deep down, was wrong and not what he wanted nor consistent with his dreams and ambitions. I know he really would have preferred a heterosexual marriage and a healthy family. (Whether he was ever sexually abused as a child, I do not know. It would not surprise me if he was, since evidence shows that such abuse is often a contributing factor.)

Finally, I want to make it clear that in this book I am *judging no one*, neither in motives or behavior. I can't peer into people's hearts. Nor is that my desire. The judgments I make here have solely to do with the question of acceptable Christian behavior according to divine revelation. I leave room for others' interpretations, and don't question their motives.

What I present here is what I believe and what I teach. I think it is a true interpretation and application of Scripture. But I speak with no authority other than to point people to the Word of God. There we find truth and grace, instruction and correction; love and truth wrapped together and revealed most perfectly in Jesus Christ.

People who view homosexual behavior as acceptable for Christians will likely reject the distinction between a judgment about doctrine and a judgment about persons. I understand that. But as a Jesus-follower, I feel responsible to interpret Scripture as faithfully as I can for myself and others.

Finally, each person is left before God with his or her conscience, and the conscience of the community to which he or she belongs.

If the church bans homosexual behavior as acceptable Christian practice, isn't it further oppressing an already persecuted minority? Some people say it is. But no, just the opposite. The faithful church champions full freedom in Christ for *everyone*—victory over the shackles of sin. In so doing the Christian community defends the rights and freedom of the Christian minority in the fact of a dominant culture which wants to squeeze the church into its own mold.

I conclude with Jesus' reminder: "If you belonged to the world, the world would love you as its own. But you do not belong to the world, for I have chosen you out of the world" (John 15:19, paraphrased).

And this, from the apostle Paul in Philippians 4:8–9: "Finally, beloved, whatever is true, whatever is honorable, whatever is just, whatever is pure, whatever is pleasing, whatever is commendable, if there is any excellence and if there is anything worthy of praise, think about these things. Keep on doing the things that you have learned and received and heard and seen in me, and the God of peace will be with you."

"Blessed be the God and Father of our Lord Jesus Christ, who has blessed us in Christ with every spiritual blessing in the heavenly places, just as he chose us in Christ before the foundation of the world to be holy and blameless before him in love" (Eph. 1:3–4).

Seven Summary Points

1. Jesus Christ is our teacher, example, and healer, as well as Savior and Lord. We should follow his lead in dealing with our own behavior and in our relationships with other people, whoever they may be.

2. With homosexuality, as with other ethical concerns, the key issue is not desire or preference or "orientation," but behavior.

3. The Bible is not unclear regarding homosexual practice. Biblical fidelity and sound interpretation require viewing homosexual practice as sinful and a violation of God's law.

4. Biblical fidelity also requires unlimited compassion and understanding towards people who experience same-sex attraction—extended in the spirit of Jesus and with the sensitivity and power of the Holy Spirit.

5. As Christians, our key identity is not based on gender or sex but rather on our life in Jesus Christ, Head and body. In Christ we find a higher and deeper identity than gender identity, yet one that sanctifies our sexuality.

6. Christians should allow no double standard in Christian obedience, but rather affirm God's call to holiness in every dimension of our lives as we seek together to follow Jesus.

7. We still have more to learn in our understanding of homosexuality and of how to deal with same-sex attraction in the church and in society.

Discussion Questions

Introduction

1. How did Jesus treat people who many in his day considered sinners or outcasts?

2. Why did Jesus say to the woman taken in adultery (John 8:1-11), "Go home, but don't sin anymore"?

3. In what ways does Jesus' example in such instances provide guidance for how we relate to persons who may be practicing homosexuals?

Section One: Four Key Biblical and Theological Considerations

1. In what ways does the Bible view homosexuality as fundamentally different from the issues of slavery and women's roles?

2. Why are stable families and the raising of children important considerations when we deal with issues of same-sex marriage?

3. Do biblical teachings on human creation in the image of God, male and female, give us guidance on the issue of homosexuality?

4. In contemporary society, is it countercultural for Christians to uphold the teaching and practice of heterosexual rather than same-sex marriage? Why is this so, and why is it significant?

5. How can Christians who adhere to the biblical standard of heterosexual marriage and families be a positive witness in society today?

6. How can Christians show unlimited love and compassion for homosexual persons while not accepting the legitimacy of same-sex unions?

Section Two: Core Issue versus Essential Doctrine

1. Is the biblical prohibition of homosexual practice an essential Christian doctrine?

2. Why did Jesus not explicitly address the question of homosexuality?

3. Do you agree with John Stott's summary of biblical teaching on gender and marriage on page 20?

4. Are biblical teachings on homosexuality and same-sex unions still relevant and applicable today?

5. Can a person endorse homosexual practice without compromising the authority of the Bible?

Section Three: Biblical Case Study

1. Are biblical teachings on homosexuality scant or unclear?

2. If some Old Testament laws no longer apply today (such as restrictions on clothing), why should not Old Testament teachings on homosexuality be disregarded today?

3. Does the Bible prohibit homosexual desires, or only homosexual behavior?

4. How does the biblical call to holiness apply to issues of homosexuality?

5. Does the fact that Christians today live in a different cultural context from New Testament Christians mean that the prohibition on same-sex unions no longer applies?

Section Four: Holy Homosexuals?

1. Is it possible for practicing homosexuals to be sincere Christians?

2. Does sincerity of Christian faith guarantee correct doctrine?

3. Same-sex attraction may have some genetic basis. If so, what does this mean for our views of homosexual practice?

4. What role does the strong emphasis on sex in contemporary society play in how young people develop their own sexual identity?

5. How should we evaluate the "accommodationist" view that, although same-sex unions are not God's original plan, they should be accepted today, given that we live in a fallen world?

6. Can abstinence from homosexual practice be a means of spiritual growth for people who experience same-sex attraction?

Section Five: Questions, Answers, More Questions

1. Can Christians who do not accept the legitimacy of homosexual practice show love to homosexuals without condemning or judging them?

2. Why have Christians and Christian churches so often rejected and condemned persons who experience same-sex attraction or engage in homosexual behavior?

3. How can our churches do a better job of nurturing and discipling persons who struggle with issues of sexual identity and who may experience same-sex attraction?

4. As Christians, how should we view (and relate to) Christians who accept homosexual practice and who often show great love and compassion toward the poor and marginalized?

5. How should we relate to people who argue that the Bible properly interpreted does not prohibit homosexual practice?

Notes

Introduction

1. Jeff Chu, *Does Jesus Really Love Me? A Gay Christian's Pilgrimage in Search of God in America* (New York: HarperCollins, 2013). My review of Chu's book can be accessed at http://howardsnyder.seedbed.com/2013/09/19/homosexuality-does-jesus-really-love-me/.

2. John Stott, *Issues Facing Christians Today*, 4th ed. (Grand Rapids: Zondervan, 2006), 446.

Section One

1. William J. Webb, *Slaves, Women & Homosexuals: Exploring the Hermeneutics of Cultural Analysis* (Downers Grove, IL: InterVarsity, 2001), 83.

2. Ibid.

3. Ibid., 252 (emphasis in the original). Stott briefly examines the issue of Scripture in relation to culture on this issue in *Issues Facing Christians Today*, 4th ed. (Grand Rapids: Zondervan, 2006), 459–60.

4. Gender (male/female) is also fundamental to human identity, but gender roles in society are largely culturally determined.

5. "See to it that no one takes you captive through hollow and deceptive philosophy, which depends on human tradition and the basic

principles of this world rather than on Christ" (Col. 2:8 NIV). "Do not be conformed to this world, but be transformed by the renewing of your minds, so that you may discern what is the will of God—what is good and acceptable and perfect" (Rom. 12:3). (All direct biblical quotations are from the NRSV unless otherwise indicated.)

6. Howard A. Snyder with Joel Scandrett, *Salvation Means Creation Healed: The Ecology of Sin and Grace: Overcoming the Divorce between Earth and Heaven* (Eugene, OR: Wipf and Stock, 2011) esp. pp. 79–80, 119–20, 155–56.

7. It is hard to imagine that compromise on the homosexuality issue will not lead to unhealthy compromises in other areas as well. In the Bible, sexual sin is often associated with idolatry.

8. Thomas Hopko, *Christian Faith and Same-Sex Attraction: Eastern Orthodox Reflections* (Chesterton, IN: Conciliar Press, 2006).

9. Ibid.

Section Two

1. John Nolland, "Romans 1:26–27 and the Homosexuality Debate," *Horizons in Biblical Theology* 22:1 (2000), 32. Nolland is referring to John Boswell, *Christianity, Social Tolerance, and Homosexuality* (1980), but the point applies more generally. Nolland adds, incidentally: "Paul's inclusion of female homoeroticism [i.e., homosexual practice, in Rom. 1:26–27] is likely to be related to the seriousness with which he took the situation of women, in light of the gospel" (54).

2. Excellent summaries are found in Stott, *Issues Facing Christians Today*, 448–54; Joe Culumber, "The Bible and Homosexuality" (unpublished paper, Greenville College, 2012, 17 pp.); and Canon Brett Cane, "The Bible and Homosexuality" (Winnipeg, Manitoba, Canada, n.d., 19 pp.), available from the author at bcane@mts.net. Another very helpful resource is the brief book by Jonathan Mills, *Love, Covenant and Meaning* (Vancouver, B.C., Canada: Regent College Publishing, 1997). James Zahniser and his colleagues help-fully bring informed psychological as well as biblical insights to bear in J. H. Zahniser and L. Cagle, "Homosexuality: Toward an informed,

compassionate response," *Christian Scholar's Review* 36 (2007), 323–48, and James H. Zahniser and Craig A. Boyd, "The Work of Love, the Practice of Compassion and the Homosexual Neighbor," *Journal of Psychology and Christianity* 27:3 (2008), 215–26.

3. See John R. W. Stott, "Romans 1 and Homosexuality," posted by David Virtue on VirtueOnline, June 1, 2007, http://www.virtueonline .org/portal/modules/news/article.php?storyid=6094#.Ul67rS4o5jo.

Section Three

1. John Nolland, "Romans 1:26–27 and the Homosexuality Debate," *Horizons in Biblical Theology* 22:1 (2000), 48. Nolland is referring specifically to verse 14, but the same is true of the whole passage.

Section Four

1. John Stott, *Issues Facing Christians Today*, 4th ed. (Grand Rapids: Zondervan, 2006), 445. See also Stanton L. Jones and Mark A. Varhouse, *Ex-gays? A Longitudinal Study of Religiously Mediated Change in Sexual Orientation* (Downers Grove, IL: IVP Academic, 2007), 31–33.

2. John Wenham, *Facing Hell: An Autobiography 1913–1996* (Carlisle, UK: Paternoster, 1998), 32.

3. Stanton L. Jones and Mark A. Yarhouse, *Ex-gays? A Longitudinal Study of Religiously Mediated Change in Sexual Orientation* (Downers Grove, IL: IVP Academic, 2007).

4. Ibid., 387.

5. Rosaria Champagne Butterfield, "My Train Wreck Conversion," *Christianity Today*, January–February 2013, 111–12. See also Mario Bergner, *Setting Love in Order: Hope and Healing for the Homosexual* (Baker, 1995).

6. F. L. Cross and E. A. Livingston, eds., *The Oxford Dictionary of the Christian Church*, 3rd ed. (Oxford, UK: Oxford University Press, 1997), 10. Accommodation in this sense has some similarities with what today is called contextualization in Christian mission.

7. Ibid.

8. William Stacy Johnson, *A Time to Embrace: Same-Gender Relationships in Religion, Law, and Politics* (Grand Rapids, MI: Eerdmans, 2006), 63.

9. http://homebrewedchristianity.com/author/dr-frank-tupper/. Accessed 2/18/14.

10. Ibid.

11. There is a wide psychological and anthropological literature on "social deviance" regarding sexuality, psychological differences, and other areas, some of which maintains that "traditional societies" generally had ways of dealing with such differences through culturally recognized special roles.